One More Miracle

One More

Miracle

What Place Do Miracles Have in a Technological World?

Kenneth Foley

WESTBOW
P R E S S®
A DIVISION OF THOMAS NELSON
& ZONDERVAN

WestBow Press books may be ordered through booksellers or by contacting:

WestBow Press
A Division of Thomas Nelson & Zondervan
1663 Liberty Drive
Bloomington, IN 47403
www.westbowpress.com
1 (866) 928-1240

ISBN: 978-1-5127-7668-3 (sc)
ISBN: 978-1-5127-7670-6 (hc)
ISBN: 978-1-5127-7669-0 (e)

Library of Congress Control Number: 2017902976

Print information available on the last page.

WestBow Press rev. date: 3/3/2017

Introduction

If you could wish for a miracle, what would it be? Would you settle for one more miracle? It's a question that most of us would hesitate to answer because we may never think much about asking for miracles in this day. But supposing you had the power to ask God for a miracle, and suppose you believed he would hear you, what would you ask for? I must first assume you have some belief that God exists (and not only exists but does not have a problem with his hearing). Even if you said the prayer in your head and not out loud, would he hear you? Most people pray in this manner, silently or to themselves. They may bow their head or look up to where they believe God is and begin to pray. Back to the question: What would you pray for? You might pray for riches or power, sort of like asking the genie in the lamp to give you three wishes. I once worked with a man who didn't believe in God. I asked him what would it take to make him believe in God.

His answer surprised me: "If God left a million dollars on my porch tonight, and I opened the door and it was there on my porch, I would believe."

I asked, "Is that what it would take to make you believe in God?"

His answer was a very certain, "Yes, I would believe then."

I simply said, "Then I will pray that God does just that: I will pray that God leaves the one million dollars on your porch tonight."

The man was surprised; his eyes grew wide, and he said, "You really believe God would do that?"

I said, "Yes, I do—because you are worth a million dollars."

He came back just before we got off work and said, "I changed my mind. I don't believe God would put the money there, so don't pray and expect me to believe."

I was surprised but had left it with God what he would do regarding the money. I was ready to ask God on his behalf. It may sound crazy to believe in miracles, but in an unpredictable world where you are constantly seeing changes, how do you not believe in God? I am not suggesting you ask God for a million dollars because the Bible tells us not to tempt the Lord thy God. I leave the answer to you, whether you would ask for untold wealth or power. You might wish to become in charge of your company, your city, your county, or your state, or you may even want to become president. There is power; then there is unlimited power. How much would you ask for? That's between you and God, remembering that you should not tempt him. You might ask God for something else: perhaps a mansion with servants and automobiles and conveniences at every turn. This miracle might be possible with the help of other miracles along the way. It might be that you would have to pray and ask God for a miracle.

Jesus said, "I go to prepare a mansion for you"; therefore, that miracle will take place when you go to heaven (providing you believe in God and heaven). If God made the world and the stars and planets, your mansion would be but a blink of his eye. There are other miracles you could ask for, such as protection. You might need protection, depending on where you live and other circumstances. The Bible says he will give his angels charge over you. You may already be protected, and that's just an everyday miracle that you can count on just because he loves you.

This book is written in the hope that you will use it to guide yourself through forty days of possible miracles. Every day, you can ask God for one miracle to take place. You can use your own list or pick a miracle you feel is more appropriate for you, then pray for that miracle to take place. Just like the person I worked with, some people would be happy if God left them a large sum of money on their doorstep, but like him, they might expect it came from some unknown source and not God. What will it take for us to believe God exists and hears our prayers?

This book is written to help you with one of the most amazing powers known to humanity. Miracles have been happening for thousands of years, yet in today's technological world, we have come to rely on our electronic devices, such as computers and cell phones. A miracle might never occur until an emergency or some disaster beyond our control happens. Then we turn to God and ask for a miracle, hoping that he will hear us because we expect God to hear us when we are in physical danger.

You need to begin by believing that he exists; then, humbly ask him to please hear your prayer. Perhaps it has been a long time since you prayed. You may need to ask forgiveness for doubting that he would help you. You may need to speak to God out loud, asking him sincerely to hear you because without a doubt he loves you.

You should stay in contact with God daily. By contact, I mean prayer of some sort. Many people throughout the world pray daily; it is not the fact that they pray but that they have a relationship with God that transcends their doubts about his existence. You may believe that you are unworthy when, in fact, none of us are worthy by ourselves. It is in that feeling of unworthiness that we begin to pray, for you didn't carve out the seas; you were not there when the mountains were born. You may not realize it, but God is all powerful as well as all knowing; he knows your need before you pray. He has the power to bring forth a miracle and knows how to get it done in his own way. You must still ask God for a miracle, even though he has foreknowledge of your request.

Would you ask God for the miracle of an easier life, in which you could live much more comfortably and with less effort? Technology seems to be moving us in the right direction. Today's technology is an amazing thing; you may already rely on it far more than you realize. Hopefully, you don't rely on technology so much that you think you don't need God. Technology should not interfere with your belief in God; in fact, it should make you realize that there are things that exist that you don't control or even know about yet. Your unbelief may come from someone you know and respect who doesn't believe in God. Someone once said there are no atheists in foxholes. When the need arises for God, we believe in him the most. You don't need to be shown who God is when your needs are great enough or when your own life (or that of someone dear to you) is hanging in the balance. For most people, that's when they seek God. I am suggesting a sort of miracle savings account be built up with God, and when you really need him, your faith will be much stronger; perhaps that will make the difference in those moments when all you can do is hope and pray he hears you.

You must find God by yourself; through prayer, you will see for yourself that he answers prayers. This will increase your faith that he is real. Look around for evidence of his creation in a nice sunset or in a beautiful flower or in the wings of a butterfly. You may look to science as well for a belief in God. Who made gravity or oxygen or the stars or our bodies function so perfectly? You may even see the forgiveness of God in the eyes of your pet. There is no condemnation to a pet that only wants you to be happy.

We take pride in the devices we use today. Cell phones, emails, and text messages are very important to us. Medical devices save lives every day; businesses and governments rely on devices. We send people into space with the hope that one day we will establish colonies on the moon or Mars or some distant planet. Technology is moving faster and faster, and our dependence on technology grows exponentially as we get better devices. We may be on the brink of the next great technological advance and not even know what it is. Maybe we need a miracle of technology from God (even though we may not admit it came from him).

We are but children in a world that lies ahead of us, designed not for children or the faint of heart or the weak of mind. We will need intelligence, and intelligence comes from the minds of intelligent people. We also need faith, and that must come from the hearts of those who believe and pray. Pray that what we have not received all the technology we are to be given by God. Pray that he will pour out his blessings upon us so greatly that in the world of tomorrow, we will look upon today as being scientifically backward. Pray that it will not vanish soon and that we will require a miracle to even get back to where we are. Since miracles require prayer, why not pay it forward (even though we need to take the time to pray for it to even maintain what we now have)? The question becomes, will God hear us and not only maintain the technology we have but allow us to advance as a civilization beyond our imagination?

Take a moment during each day to ask that he allow us to continue upward on our quest to the stars and beyond. Pray for the miracle to remain ever more intelligent to be able to use the technological devices available to us. Progress requires highly intelligent people who are capable of learning large amounts of information quickly and knowing how to use it for your betterment and for the betterment of humanity. It requires mature, capable people who create advanced technology to do so with the unselfish intent of not using it to hold us hostage to that which comes forth. For example, an entire city could be held hostage if someone hacked into the water supply system of a great city.

Our greatest fear should be those within our technology systems who are capable of evil beyond what we can imagine. Future technology remains very vulnerable to these madmen who pretend to be highly intelligent but are in fact psychotic (or at the very least greedy). Imagine our military being dependent upon a system of technology that one individual could destroy in a few minutes, leaving thousands of soldiers at the mercy of an enemy whose only intent is to destroy and take what is not theirs.

Maintaining a job will likely require intelligence to operate highly advanced computers or robotic devices. Using technology, some people will become very wealthy fast, while other people are just satisfied to use technology as it comes along. You may be the one who develops the next popular program. You may be artistic and create something interesting using technology. Children learn to operate computers very young now. Young people will find many jobs because they grew up in a technological society, and it is second nature to them. As you age, will your mind slow down and your ability to use technology go away? What then is missing from this equation? Do you need more of God in your life? Do you need a miracle now in a personal way? Are personal miracles possible? Will a loving God give us miracles?

We as a civilization have relied on miracles in the past, and now we rely on technology. Has the sociological aspect of technology advanced beyond our ability to live together peacefully? Are we missing a key piece of the puzzle? We are moving closer to weapons beyond our imagination; can it be that the missing piece of the puzzle is God's help? If we have God by then, why would we worry? Are we incapable of advancing into the future based upon our need for a relationship with God? Are we incapable of receiving help from such an enormously intelligent being, who is way beyond our imagination? Is it possible to utilize God in a techno-driven world? What will the future be like? Is it possible that through prayer and miracles, we can help redesign the future?

The concept that God will provide all humanity with even greater technology through some miracle may seem unreal, yet you cannot be sure that you have not received miracles already in technology and throughout life. Follow the path of history, and see that inventions like copper, brass, and iron changed civilizations overnight. Now we examine the dust of the ancients and wonder why they disappeared. What happened to the mighty cities of long ago and their great armies that supposedly could conquer all that could stand before them? Just examine the last five thousand years of evolving cities and armies unto where we are today. God was there, and God is here today: the same God. Will we follow those ancient civilizations? Will people someday sift through the dust and examine what was once our great technological civilization and wonder? Or will we ask God for a miracle? Will you ask God for a miracle? We need a miracle, and God can give us that miracle.

It is as if an unseen hand did something that changed your whole way of living from your parents until today and your grandparents would never believe it possible for us to be so advanced in technology. What are you going to rely on? Will you rely on a cell phone, or will it be possible for you to make your own atomic bomb or weapon of destruction? What exactly are our capabilities? Will we proceed in peace or war? Can technology alone save you? That would take a miracle; perhaps a technological miracle that saves us will take place. It may well take a miracle to save our civilization. The miracle we need is waiting to appear, or is it already here in God? Will we rely upon God?

The technology that we will see in the very near future is so advanced that we cannot comprehend it: things from nanotechnology to quantum mechanics and robotic advances and devices that control just about everything we do. Our genetic map may even be changed because of technology. Technology is reaching out faster and faster, in hopes of the next device or cure for a disease. Is genetics the answer to the future? Will you have a longer life because of technology? Will technology help you survive longer? Good health is important. Will you become amazingly healthy in the future, using advancements in skin care and health supplements? We need the God that made us to help us. Will you rely on God's miracles to help you be happier and healthier tomorrow?

For quite some time, factories have used robots to build cars. Will a robot take your job, or will you have a robotic assistant on your job or at home? Will you carry a chip that constantly monitors your body for medical reasons? How many chips will you carry? You could have several medical monitoring devices attached to you internally or externally. Drones could be used to bring medical supplies or aid to you if you have an accident. Drones could bring you food and other goods from businesses and companies. There seems to be no limit to what technology can bring us. You may park your automobile (or other transport device) on a miniature power grid that enables you to energize your mode of transportation almost instantly. There may be devices that energize your body, with or without food. Food may be completely different then; it may have an unbelievable taste without calories. By just swallowing a pill, you may feel a surge of energy, or the pill itself may be able to energize you for days, weeks, and even years. Food supply may be a problem, but technology may just be up to the challenge. There may be pills that genetically alter your body or give you new and different skills. You may suddenly be able to sing or dance or do acrobatics, things that you never could do before simply by swallowing a pill. Technology is taking us to new worlds, but without God, you may be like a wobbling tire that eventually falls off because it has lost the bolts that hold it on. We expect our tires to stay on. Why not expect God to hold our world together with miracles every day?

You need the help of God, now and in the future. Imagine a world that has no way to power its technology. Power grids may break down with age or overloaded circuitry. God must protect you also when the weather becomes a threat. You need God to protect you in weather-related situations. Because of Doppler radar, there have been fewer airplane accidents. Technology has rescued us, but supposing instruments began to work differently on cars and airplanes and other forms of transportations. Most cars today have several computers. Computers rely upon the laws of physics, and they are basically controlled by God. You should pray that God will continue being generous to us as his children. Expect God to protect us through prayer and miracles.

We have seen comets and meteors come close to the earth. We can pray to the God of the heavens and ask for protection from any danger we may face on earth or as we travel beyond our planet or simply live in time and space not knowing our future.

God can control diseases that could become dangerous in the future. We have seen flu seasons that seem to go into extreme conditions and finally left us after weeks of struggling. Perhaps you have had experience with colds, flu, or allergies or other ailments. It is very possible with God's help to be safe from future ailments of any kind that can occur beyond our control. We don't even know what caused the dinosaur to be become extinct. Do we have value as a civilization? Are we meant to worship God but have lost the way? We are not primitive like the ancients, and we know that prayer changes things. Ancient civilizations raised children for a purpose: to be sacrificed for the good of the people. We serve a God who is far above any other idol or god of the past. It is up to us to look to God and worship his might and power and to know he loves us. As individuals, we need to worship God and ask for miracles of every kind.

You may have a list of miracles you seek that you have used for a long time; hopefully, you will want to add these forty miracles to your list, or you may find new miracles to pray for. Possibly you have never prayed for a miracle or maybe you don't know how to pray. The devotional prayer program is just a suggestion; you may choose to pick your favorite miracle that you want God to do. With miracles, you may rebuild your world; you and future generations will greatly benefit from prayer. Speak to God as a friend and ask that you might be given a miracle.

It is not a competition, where technology is versus God. We are not in a match for who wins, science or God. Hopefully, you will look to both technology and God. God is a mighty and super intelligent being, and you will benefit from his greatness, his holiness, and the unseen power that he has at his control. In a new world where miracles can occur, dangers flee from us because we have already prayed for God's intervention. In a world where storms are turned from their course or diseases are brought under control, we grow exponentially as a civilization. We don't become part of a dream world where we allow days, weeks, and years to go by and then disaster strikes. Hopefully, we live in a world of peaceful unity. You may gain from reading this book by applying it to your daily life. You may see God differently, not as a gray-haired old man but a living God who is as young today as he was when he created Earth and Mars and the other planets and stars. Your future may not lie in the next device you purchase but in the next prayer that affects your daily life or the life of someone you know or someone in a distant country. Does the future lie in your prayers and the prayers of others? Do we want to take a chance on the future being alright because it's alright at this moment? Do we know the future?

Someday, you may need a miracle just to walk down the street safely. It may not be safe where you live today after dark. That's not a step forward for civilization. If you live or work in that type of community, or you shop in it, you must pray for a miracle to get you from place to place safely. Pray also that God will remove the frightening aspects of your neighborhoods and cities. The enemy can be deceptive; just be aware of deceptions that come along into your daily life. Be strong through God by asking for his help and protection. Just pray as you go through life every day. Whenever you see the need for God to help, you need to pay attention and pray for protection from whatever frightens you or could cause you the slightest harm. Miracles can occur, and that's what we need: miracle awareness, not just blind faith. Pray for God to give you a miracle over such things and to be protected everywhere you go. Other people in your neighborhood need prayer as well as yourself. Pray for others as well as yourself.

In foreign countries, religious persecution is common. Be aware that when you go to other countries, you could suffer persecution from people who don't understand your God and the way he helps you. God will protect you and deliver you out of the hand of any enemy, even out of prison. Just being aware of the country you travel to could save you from unseen dangers and unpredictable events. It is better to take God with you on a trip than to call upon him later, wondering why he didn't help. Pray for those who would cause you harm. Tell them about your God when you feel the time is right.

Soon, scientists may take us to Mars and beyond. They will quite likely be able to establish a colony on Martian soil within your lifetime. Who would have ever thought it possible for us to even travel to Mars? Will we need God to help us dig under the red planet's soil? What could go wrong with such a difficult mission? Who can help if trouble occurs on the way? What about after they have landed and grown their own food and find things under the soil? Do we need God even in space? The truth is that every time we go into space, something new ends up being a product that we find on the shelf later. The space program has provided us with much in technology. You may have not noticed that technology and miracles coincide more often than you think. We have no idea how may products there are that have come from space technology. Things that are common for space travel will likely become common on earth. What protects them will protect us, and what supplies them will supply us; they will go hand in hand.

Much of It began in the minds of science fiction writers, or even before that, when ancient humans looked up at the moon and wondered. Some civilizations worshiped the moon and the planets, places where we will soon travel to. Then they began to see Gods in the wind and rain and all of nature. Most every culture in history has had some form of God; superstitions reigned and then became pagan rituals. Superstitions still are common today, most baseball players refuse to step on the lines between home plate and first or third base when they enter or leave the field. You may have some form of superstition, such as glasses cannot touch when they are in the cabinet or a black cat crossing in front of you is bad luck. But miracles go beyond those beliefs. Miracles are a form of answer to prayer if we choose to pray. Regardless of your beliefs, it is necessary to ask God for your daily needs; ask him for blessings every day. The greatest blessing you can ask for is a miracle. It may be difficult to describe a miracle, but it is an act of God that can't be explained. By all we know, it could not have happened except for divine intervention. When you ask for a miracle, you must realize that a miracle will happen if God chooses for it to happen. Don't take credit for any miracles that occur because God is a jealous God, and if he performs a miracle, it will be his decision to do so, when he chooses to do it. You might say it's God's little secret, but he is able. He can move heaven and earth. God can destroy any plagues or bacteria or diseases or enemies that may threaten us or our country. Technology will seem small to you when you see God's way of doing miracles. It's not like you can go to a website and push a button; it must be a prayer to God personally.

> Believing is the engine that drives our prayers.
> Faith lays them at the foot of the throne of God.
> Hope becomes the expectation of a miracle.
> Trust is the belief that God hears our request, and
> the miracle begins.

It is now that God shows himself to us in a world we never knew existed. It is here that life is made better than it was in the darkness of the night. It is here the sun begins to come out from behind the clouds, and a rainbow appears. It is here a baby looks up and smiles. It is here we receive a God-given miracle, all because we asked for it. It is here that technology becomes less important, and the only thing that matters is that God has moved, and a miracle has taken place.

Without miracles that come forth from his world, your daily life could be catastrophic. You may find yourself someday discarding many devices because of security or other reasons, but never discard God because the darkest hours become filled with light when he hears your prayer. It is in the darkest hours of our life we often turn to God and only then that we ask him to intercede.

The answer to your future may not be beneath the soil of Mars; it may lie in the quiet solitude of your place of prayer. Where you choose to pray does not matter. The fact that you do pray, regardless of all the technology you have, is a miracle. As you venture into the unknown of space, who is to say which is greater: technology or God? Can technology wipe God from our hearts and minds? No. Can God wipe technology from our hearts and minds? God can do anything he chooses. It is God's grace that allows us to travel safely anywhere.

In the world to come, will you need technology? When there is no need for technology in the holy place of God, where no shadows exist, in the place where your eternal soul will dwell, technology will disappear. Until that day, you will hunger for that which consoles you. You live in the land of mortals and seek a God who is immortal for miracles. Will you rely upon technology when the heavens roll back and you see the face of God? You are in a place no man or woman has ever been. You are in a world where one nuclear submarine can defend your freedom, but with God, it may only be necessary to pray that it is not needed. You need a miracle for humans to survive and move forward to a world God filled with the wonders of technology. Together, we can endure the future and rejoice in one miracle after another, as God sees fit to give them to us. The future lies ahead of us and through prayer it can be wonderful.

In a world that is not far away, you can ask for God's hand to guide you through the narrows of uncertainty into a new world of technology and miracles. He will lead you forward as you live in a world secured by his hand. Are you at the stage where you need one more miracle? Have you found the pathway that leads to peace in a world of hunger? God can save the lives of millions of people with one prayer. Is one prayer worth saying? Is a prayer that comes from deep inside you, that asks God to stop destruction, hard to say? To neglect such a prayer is to not believe that God can make the world anew, with technology by our side. What a waste it would be to stop now on the brink of a new world that we can only hope is blind to color, or race, or nationality, or religion. What a waste to not pray, not being quite sure if God will hear you. What a waste of humanity not to turn to God at this pivotal time in history, when he can bring peace and great blessings upon the earth. God can feed the starving and cure the greatest of illnesses. What a waste to not pray when so much power is given to us through Gods miracles.

Peace and goodwill amongst all men can and must come forth.

From beneath the throne of God can come rivers of living waters. Miracles, like a long life, can come to a world that has almost forgotten where miracles come from. You need a miracle beyond your mind's imagination. You need a miracle that's stronger than your hopelessness. It is sad to think that humanity will destroy itself. It is not necessary to even think about possible things that can go bump in the night. Only God can know the future, and you should not assume that he will allow terrible things to happen to us. Believe and pray and trust by faith that you can be reborn in peace. The idea that God created us all just to destroy us is staggering. A God who loves us would not allow such a thing to happen. Pray for a miracle; pray that you may find the ear of God, as did saints of old. May he hear your prayers and welcome them and return miracles untold into your life. May tomorrow bring much happiness; we will all breathe a little easier in a world where technology has become so advanced and wonderful, we say, "Thank you," to God.

Can you but find peace, happiness, and joy through God's miracles? Find the ancient doorway of the past, where saints prayed and came before God's throne, humbly asking him for help and miracles. Find the future in your prayer of a world so vast and wonderful that the angels sing with humanity. In tomorrow's world, which brings together technology with God, may your happiness cup be full and running over. May you find One More Miracle somehow that makes the world a better place and makes your life a little safer and more worthwhile.

Let us pray.

Day 1

Pray for all the people in the world who need to receive a miracle from God today. Pray that today, someone will receive a miracle that is unexpected but will bring them joy, happiness, or healing.

Sometimes, you may feel as if you are the only one in the world. You may even feel that nobody cares about you. You cannot put a face on someone, but the reality is that the world is full of people just like you. People exist in all colors, races, and nationalities. You may mentally block out people or world conditions by staying busy. You may block the needs of others because you feel they don't care about you or even know you. You may stay busy and feel somebody else needs to take care of the world, thinking, it's not my job, and ignore the world you live in. You may have all you can handle on your plate right now and feel the problems of the world belong to the United Nations or some group that specializes in that sort of thing.

The truth is that many people still go to bed hungry at night. Some have cuts, bruises, and sores. There may be no medical help for the deathly ill where they live, or they may not have the money to pay for a doctor. They may have lost all hope. Fortunately, there are volunteers who try to help them, but they are too few, and there are just too many people to help. Those are the kind of people who need a miracle. They may not even know that there is a God who can help them.

Your belief in God is a powerful tool. To look to God with faith and prayer is to help people who don't know God, for if they did, they might begin to worship him. Could it be that the greatest riches you have are in God? Could your belief in miracles be a source of wealth to the world? Could it be that technology is not the greatest power in the world? Could it be that the future of our world lies not just in technology and all its attributes, but also in the miracles that God can give you every day? Is it possible to have both technology and God?

When you look upon children, the elderly, and the lame, do you feel something? Do you hope that technology can eradicate hunger and disease? When you feel that for just a moment, you need to pray that God will send a miracle. If you believe it is possible that a miracle could take place, then ask God for a miracle at that moment. You may not see the miracle that takes place, but one can take place in an instant. Time and space with God are beyond our comprehension. A God who hears your prayer may do something to help the person you pray for. When you pray, do you go beyond technology into a world unknown to you? Prayer is a powerful force, and you have that power if you just pray for a miracle.

If you have the power and capability to pray, and you believe God performs miracles, you have a power that's greater than any other in the world. You may not have known you have such an awesome power available to you. Some people claim they are the only ones capable of praying for such miracles, but they deceive you out of your power. Who would do such a thing as that? It is no wonder people of other religions think of us as greedy and selfish when we just have never exercised the greatest power known to humanity. Other nations that are not as blessed as ours wonder why we are blessed. They don't just need our dollars; they need our prayers.

Be thankful for your own blessings, but remember the people who don't know God. Remember to pray that God will bless them with food, medical help, technology, and understanding. You serve a powerful God who hears your prayers and can hear theirs as well. Open your heart to those less fortunate and ask God for one more miracle in the life of someone you have never met (and most likely will never meet). Pray for a miracle to come to that person as an unexpected gift; let it come as a complete surprise.

How could we verify that such a miracle took place? We couldn't. In fact, this might take us out of the realm of determining who gets blessed or is healed or receives a miracle. Let God be God, and let the power be in his hands. We need only pray, and our job is finished. Let God do the rest. How difficult could that be? Don't be surprised if God somehow creates a miracle in your life because you remembered someone else, and a miracle took place because of your love for others.

"This is my commandment: that ye love one another, as I have loved you" (John 15:12 KJV).

Day 2

Pray that weapons of mass destruction will never be used anywhere in the world. Pray that God will intervene and prevent such a thing from happening to anyone in the world.

It may be quite easy for you to say, "At least it didn't happen here in this country." Then came September 11, and you saw what can happen—not just in some distant land. The thing you may have feared happened, and perhaps something worse could happen in the future. Major wars happen in other countries and cities around the world.

The reason to pray for a miracle of such gigantic proportions is that all the world may suffer if one suffers. You are aware every day of how technology has linked us together. There is no longer just a theory of globalized trade; we live in a world where one part of an automobile or airplane may be made in one part of the world and another part is made far across the globe. If one country suffers an enormous devastation from bombs or missiles, we could all suffer greatly.

You may not be able to imagine the difficulty that could occur if, for example, a major automaker was destroyed and you could no longer get parts for your car. It might take years to rebuild that factory. Consequently, a car could break down on a major highway, stalling traffic indefinitely because of one part. You are aware that you live in a dangerous and unpredictable world and need a plan to survive. The plan you need is God. Look to a miracle. God does not manufacture miracles; he simply speaks them into existence. It is hard to imagine such a powerful God. Yet in the beginning was the word, which is beyond our understanding. You speak to devices, and things happen, so you are living in a world you hope doesn't crumble. You must first look to God for peace and understanding. To pray and ask God for a miracle of this magnitude may be beyond your ability to comprehend. You can, however, ask God for such a miracle, believing he will hear your prayer.

There are big and small miracles. I would put most in the classification of big miracles— do not hesitate to ask God for big miracles. When you look at pictures taken by the Hubble telescope, you cannot help being in awe and wonder. How could so much space be filled with stars and beautiful galactic sights? Yet the same God made our earth—and he made you. It sounds much easier to believe in the big bang. Would it make a difference what God used to create all things or how he put things in such magnificent order?

The word "magical" comes to mind. Thinking of God as a great magician might make you more comfortable in understanding him, but God's magic is real, not an illusion. Much of what you may see is real. From our imagination came technology, which means God helped create it. Can you imagine a world without technology or imagination? Your future is based upon the imaginations of those who can invent new technological devices, and what you see today will quite likely change, just as other things change in nature. If God gave you the technology you have, then you must realize that his love is something you may not understand. Yet it is God who gave you a technological future based upon imagination and those of others capable of such powers. You may see stage after stage of technology, and your imagination must accept the God-given technology that changes often and realize his gift.

You may simply ask God for continued peace among all nations and to prevent a disastrous end to all that your world consists of. You can simply ask God to protect you and the rest of the world by performing a miracle. God is not a God who performs tricks, like you might ask of a dog. God is holy and to be revered. If you can simply pray to prevent great future calamities, you would perform a wonderful service to humanity. Your voice may be only one voice, but one voice has been known to cause miracles before. Ask God for one more miracle that will keep your planet safe. Pray that God will not allow such a thing to happen to you or the world that he made because he loves you.

"In the beginning was the Word, and the Word was with God, and the Word was God. The same was in the beginning with God. All things were made by him; and without him was not anything made that was made" (John 1:1–3 KJV).

Day 3

Pray for a cure for diseases in general; whatever disease comes to mind, pray that God will provide the cure for it through science and miracles and that it won't come back. Pray also that new diseases that are in the beginning stages of development somewhere in the world will be eliminated.

We are indeed fortunate to have cures and medicines for so many diseases. Doctors can diagnose ailments using advanced technology and instruments. Transplants of organs take place quite often now. Perhaps in no other area of our world has advancement taken such giant leaps.

We trust in science and knowledge to help us survive another day or year or decade. No matter how long we live, we want doctors and scientists and research workers to continue helping us live longer and be healthier.

Yet nowhere is God more evident than in the medical field. It is almost as if God specializes in medicine. How often do we hear the words "It's up to God now"? In one of humanity's greatest areas of achievement, we bow to God for his will to be done and realize we really need a miracle.

"Beloved, If God so loved us, we ought to love one another" (1 John 4:11 KJV).

Day 4

Pray for the miracle that God will supply humanity with another great invention that will benefit all of civilization. That invention may be in the medical field or something like the Internet or cell phone. Pray that the invention be such a blessing that it will save lives or bring food to the hungry in the world. Pray that it will greatly benefit you and your friends and family.

There have been so many inventions throughout our short time here on earth. It is difficult to single out any one invention as being greater than another. Inventions are undoubtedly one of the most important things in our lives; we rely on them daily, from refrigerators to running water, from heaters to packaging of our foods. We look on the Internet and see projected inventions and wonder what will come next; before we know what happened the whole world has changed.

Not knowing what invention will be next, pray that it will be powerful enough to make the world a better place and that our children and their children will be able to benefit from it daily.

"How much better is it to get wisdom than gold! And to get understanding rather to be chosen than silver!" (Proverbs 16:16 KJV).

Day 5

Pray for the miracle that no great disaster come upon the earth. In whatever form a disaster may take, whether it be storms or earthquakes or floods or meteors or any form of great disaster that can come upon you, pray that it will pass over you. Pray also that should a disaster occur, you will survive whatever form it takes.

Today, you have amazing access to weather information and can know ahead of time when a storm is coming. You can take shelter and be safe if you know ahead of time. That is because we have advanced as a society and civilization. Without the miracle of storm and weather detection, you would not be as safe. Aircraft now use Doppler radar to help planes land safely. The future it seems will have even more advanced early warning systems to help you go to work or take shelter at home to prepare for unseen dangers. When you pray, ask God to help you through those moments when you are unsure if you will survive. All the warning systems may not do you any good, without God's help. People still are injured or killed even if they know the danger is coming toward them. One more miracle might just save your life; protect yourself and friends and family with prayer. Ask for this miracle today.

"For whatsoever is born of God over cometh the world: and this is the victory that over cometh the world, even our faith" (1 John 5:4 KJV).

Day 6

Pray for the miracle of peace within yourself. Pray to be able to overcome the things that overwhelm you. Pray for the strength to be able to handle things and events that you cannot handle by yourself.

Sometimes, it may seem things happen when you least expect it. You go through life full of happiness and confidence, unaware that something unexpected will happen. You may feel that nobody cares or even knows what you are going through. You may have had a car accident or fell and nobody even knew about it but you. You don't necessarily wish bad things to happen to others, but you may be glad that they didn't happen to you. You may lose your job or be accused of doing something you never did. You may have come down with a terrible illness. You may lose a friend to drugs or something else, and now they are gone. We never know what other people are suffering. A divorce may happen suddenly, and it becomes more than you can handle. Things happen through no fault of your own, but you blame yourself. Pray for the miracle to overcome every difficult situation. Pray to have strength to go on with your life if they occur. Pray that if such things happen, God gives you the strength to handle them. Pray for that miracle.

"And I said, 'Oh that I had wings like a dove! For then would I fly away, and be at rest'" (Psalm 55:6 KJV).

Day 7

Pray for the gift of being able to help others. Pray for the miracle of discernment of knowing when someone else is troubled beyond their own strength. Become the strength of others through God's help.

When you are upset about something, you may wonder why no one else cares. It may just be that they don't know how badly you are hurting. One day, a friend begins to cry, and you know somehow what they feel. You may ask why they are crying. Discernment is given to some people, and you may be one of those people who can talk to a friend or coworker and let them know you care about them. You do not have to be romantically involved with them; caring goes beyond romance. In those moments when you are hurting, the touch of someone else's hand is all you need. If you care about someone, you may talk to them a long time about what has upset them. To reach out and touch someone who is suffering is a gift from God. Discernment is given to those who have feelings for others and care about them. When the day comes that you are troubled, you may find someone else will listen to you. If you want a friend, be a friend. Just having someone touch your hand and look in your eyes may be all you need. Know how to touch someone and look in their eyes and just listen until they get it all out. The fact that somebody else cares about them means a lot to them. Somebody else knows you are hurting and wants it to go away; this can become part of your way of being a friend. Be that someone who is blessed of God with discernment. Let others be your friend when you need it most as well.

You may see someone you don't know who is hurting deeply inside, and you want to just touch them and say, "I can tell something has hurt you; can I ask what it is?" What if they won't answer you? Then go on and pray for them, knowing you tried. On the other hand, you may have just let someone talk about what is hurting them badly if they will allow it and now they can get on with their life. People don't mean to be cruel, but you may be given the power of God to help in some way. You may be God's front line at that moment. It's all right to have such a privilege; through God's miracle, you can have that strength, not just for yourself but others as well. Something you say may be what they need to hear; God will tell you the words to say. Do not doubt God. Pray for that gift, but know you may feel the pain of others. You will need enough strength for that gift. You will need strength, so ask God for it. Ask God for a miracle of discernment and the strength to help others.

"He that believeth on me; as the scripture hath said, out of his belly shall flow rivers of living water" (John 7:38 KJV).

Day 8

Pray that God will provide a miracle to the elderly and injured. Pray for those who are unable to walk or who need a wheelchair to move from place to place. Pray that the elderly will be able to care for themselves, that they can walk and move their hands and hear and see and enjoy their golden years. Pray for a scientific breakthrough today somewhere in the world that can help elderly and injured people. No matter how small the miracle, may it help them somehow with their hearing or eyesight or walking or arm movements. May it bring them freedom from confinement in a nursing home or hospital or other care facility. Pray that the breakthrough will be so great that it will benefit all humanity, and if we are injured as we get older, let a miracle take place to cure us. Pray that there may be a way to perform some miracle surgery that will cause many to be saved from their ailments and suffering. These people awake to a different world than others do; they suffer every day. Pray that it will come even as a genetic breakthrough or that it will be a miracle beyond our scope of imagination. Pray that it will be something that will affect your own life in the world to come as well (or someone you love or know).

We all know that the world is in great sickness. People often use wheelchairs or canes or are all crippled up somehow. Nursing homes and hospitals are filled with sick and lame people. We have come to believe in miracles, and here we find people who need a miracle. Let your prayers begin. You may need that miracle. You may have an ailment and need God's help to get you through it. Do not forget the elderly, for as we all live longer lives, we will surely develop ailments and problems; they not only affect the elderly but soldiers who come back from the war and accident victims as well. Pray for such a miracle to come soon.

"They will perish, but you will remain, they will all wear out like a garment. Like clothing you will change them and they will be discarded. But you remain the same and your years will never end" (Psalm: 102:26–27 NIV).

Day 9

The future of all humanity is at stake. They say that an entire country can cease to exist in one hour. We have so much destructive capability among so many nations; we fear that some madman or a religious leader will unleash devastation simply because they feel God has told them it is the right thing to do. Pray for a miracle that will prevent such a calamity. Pray that day will never come. If that would happen, it would be the darkest day in history. Pray for the miracle of safety for you and your loved ones and our nation should such a thing take place. The possibility exists today that such an attack could happen. Pray for the miracle that prevents destruction upon our nation and other nations around the world.

Nobody disputes the fact that many nations today have the capability to destroy one another. The miracle is that nobody has yet done so. There are many groups of people who believe in killing simply because it is their duty to kill or destroy their enemy. Some people believe they have the right to destroy others, and they believe they can do so simply because they feel strongly about what they are doing as part of their faith. The future is a mystery because one individual could become as lethal as an entire army with a weapon of mass destruction Whatever the reason someone feels justified to kill or destroy could also be a medical reason or drugs or alcohol. The reasons could be endless. They may have experienced what they feel is an act against them that was not fair to them and they seek revenge for a relationship that failed or a work incident. No matter the reason people go off the deep end and commit acts of violence that stagger the mind. What future events will we face? Do we need to pray for God to intervene? We need to pray for those people to come to their senses before they harm someone else or harm many people for whatever the reason. God can intervene if we but pray for a miracle to take place in the mind of one person or the minds of many. Pray God will keep you safe wherever you are as well.

If we did not have God, we would have been destroyed by our enemies by now. Thankfully, we have not yet suffered that great catastrophe. We simply do not know what a day can bring. I would say woe to that nation if it be a nation, for it too would likely be destroyed along with its misguided religious belief. Pray for God to always intervene on our behalf, and pray that God will allow us all to go in peace, letting all nations live peaceably. It is our hope that we may progress into the future, one technological breakthrough at a time, one miracle at a time and that civilization will progress in peace and prosperity together. Pray for the miracle that God will not allow such a calamity of destruction to take place anywhere in the world today or in the future.

"Since no one knows the future who can tell someone else what is to come?" (Ecclesiastes 8:7 NIV).

Day 10

Pray for the miracle that starving children will find a crust of bread or food of some sort. Pray that those children will grow and become blessings to humanity and will cease to be angry for the conditions that they suffered as children.

You cannot feed the world by yourself, but you can pray for a miracle. Who can forget the miracle when Christ fed the five thousand from a few fishes and loaves of bread? People have found food in strange ways; there are many groups that make sincere efforts to feed children and adults worldwide. As the population of the world grows, the feeding of many people becomes more difficult. The thought of a starving child is difficult to absorb for those who live in a world of plenty. Yet children and adults starve to death every day. Pray God will perform a miracle today to feed such starving and hungry children and adults. Pray that technology can help the starving children and other starving people in the world as well.

"Suppose a brother or a sister is without clothes and daily food. If one of you says to them, 'Go in peace, keep warm and well fed,' but does nothing about their physical needs, what good is it?" (James 2:15–16 NIV)

Day 11

Pray that world situations do not develop into large-scale disputes or wars. Many troubled nations have disputes over small things. In time's past, wars have started over a pretty face or petty event. The reasons we have gone to war are absurd. We have fought wars over political problems which create wealth for some and destruction and poverty for others. Pray that the development of world disputes ceases today and that peace prevails before a more serious situation develops and causes the lives of many to be taken unnecessarily.

Pray for peace to prevail. It's easy to see how one nation can consider itself stronger or wiser than another. There seems to be trouble everywhere in the world over religions and freedoms and wealth and boundaries. We can pray that differences are resolved and that men live in freedom and liberty throughout the world, without the threat of imprisonment or death. Pray for the miracle of world peace. Pray that technology will help be a part of world peace.

"May the nations be glad and sing for joy. For you rule them with equity and guide the nations of the earth" (Psalm 67:4 NIV).

Day 12

Pray for a miracle to end poverty and that water will be abundant for all people. Pray God will allow us to live in a world with plenty of food and water. Technology must lead the way to a better world, not of death and destruction but of peace and plenty. Pray that people all over the world will be free from greed and jealousy of those who are wealthy and are well provided for. Pray for a miracle that provides sufficient food and water in such a way as to benefit all humanity and that you will be provided for, as well. It is natural to always look to others as a guide to what you want, but it is better to pray for enough food and water. Pray for the miracle to overcome world hunger and a world water shortage.

Many people wish they had more money. They feel they can never have enough money to buy more goods, services, and devices. You want what is best for yourself, but God can make whatever you have last sufficiently as well. Ask God for the miracle of adequate food and water.

"A ruler who lacks understanding is a great oppressor. But he who hates covetousness will prolong his days" (Proverbs 28:16 NKJV).

Day 13

Pray for the miracle that God will use you somehow in his wonderful plan to reach out to others. God does not have to call you to preach, but he may call you to work in his vineyard. He may call you to be used in some way that only you can reach someone in need. Somehow in your past, you may have had God training. You may have not even known it was God training. Now he wants you to work, and he wants to use you. Pray he will show you that miracles do work.

Sometimes, you feel downtrodden and sick about who you are and how worthless you are. You may have considered harming yourself because you are nobody in your mind, but in fact, you are somebody. Things that happened could have destroyed you, but they didn't because a miracle took place unseen by you; that miracle was for a reason. It was God saying, "I am not done using you yet. I have a plan for you." Look for it, seek it out, and pray for it to appear. Reach out and take the miracle. Run toward your own miracle. With tears in your eyes, rejoice because you have found God's plan. With joy in your heart, touch someone today with words and encouragement, for you are blessed. Let God teach you what you need to know to help others.

"For in him you have been enriched in every way—with all kinds of speech and with all knowledge" (1 Corinthians 1:5 NIV).

Day 14

Pray for the miracle to help those with drug or alcohol problems. Pray you will see beyond these people to their problems and needs. Look upon the hearts of these people who are misled and cannot stop what they are doing to themselves and others. This rampant problem is medical in nature but also spiritual as well. Look upon the faces of these children and see that they may someday be subject to drugs or alcohol. They may already be a victim. Some people devote their lives to helping those who are being destroyed by drugs and alcohol. These heroes should be rewarded. You can be one of those heroes with a simple prayer that asks for a miracle to eradicate the effects of drugs and alcohol. How many lives must be destroyed before we deal properly with these problems of the body and soul? Pray for a miracle to help rid our society of this curse upon humanity. Families are affected by this plague upon society, which is slowly killing many. If you are a victim or are on drugs or alcohol, pray for a miracle that helps you beyond your problem. Pray for a miracle. Pray for the strength to use this miracle wisely.

People put on a face that works for their job or their social life, but they may secretly be controlled by drugs or alcohol. The truth is, inside they hurt, and they hurt badly. Watch the things they do, especially the secret ways they try to hide it when someone is around them or their reaction to what you say. To them, it may hurt more than it should. Some of these people live in a world of horror, waiting for their next fix that will ease their pain. For them, the tragedy of losing a friend is horrifying; they cannot begin to grasp it or face it. Things you ordinarily do are so difficult for them to do; we cannot conceive of their struggles. We simply cannot know what they are going through; only trained people can help them, unless you have been through this nightmare yourself and understand it. Most of these people are in some sort of pain; the pain is indescribable, but they use drugs or alcohol to ease their symptoms. Talk to them and convince them to get help for their problem, but do not expect them to call soon. They may need to reach a point where God finds them and helps them; that's when a miracle takes place. Pray for the person on drugs or alcohol and ask that God will walk beside them and protect them during their battle and that he will lead them to a place where they surrender the pain to God. Pray for that miracle. Pray for their fear of being caught and given help for their fear is great.

"Therefore. as God's chosen people holy and dearly loved, clothe yourselves with compassion, kindness, humility, gentleness and patience" (Colossians 3:12 NIV).

Day 15

Pray for the miracle to bear the burdens of others. Look for someone who has lost a child or contracted some serious ailment. The world is full of heavy burdens, and we are supposed to take them to God. Help those who are heavy laden with burdens. You need not carry upon your back a load so heavy you bow under its weight; let God carry it for you. Pray to be God's helper. Pray for that miracle.

Remember that you are not a miracle maker. By yourself, you can do nothing. You call on God to do the impossible because he alone has that power. We simply ask for the miracle we cannot create it. A miracle is God doing the impossible; it might not happen unless you pray. Seek to understand the needs of others and pray for them, whether you receive credit now or in the world to come. Look for those who have lost children and pray with them and pray for them. Look for those who now have diseases that are serious and comfort them with prayer and pray for them to receive a miracle. Look for those who have given up hope and teach them to pray. Look for those who cannot face another day by themselves pray with them and for a miracle.

"The Lord is near to all who call upon him, to all who call on him in truth" (Psalm 145:18 NIV).

Day 16

Who are the wise people in our land and throughout the world? Are wise people the smartest people in the world? Does anyone listen to those who are wise? Many people in the world have the miracle of wisdom. Pray for that gift to come to you. Wisdom can save your life; it can make life much easier. Pray for the miracle of wisdom to come to you from God.

God knows the future. God knows what works. Through wisdom, God can help you choose what to buy or where to go, who to help and what to say. Wisdom from God can tell you not to get on an airplane that later goes down. Study Proverbs and see the wisdom of Solomon. Wisdom is not knowing sometimes because that can be the beginning of wisdom. Wait until you know the answer because you ask God's help, then you may be surprised what you do or say. Ask God for his wisdom to guide you. Wisdom comes from God; it must come from God. No matter how intelligent you are, you just can't manufacture wisdom. You may have a high SAT score but can't make good decisions. You need God's wisdom, especially in this age of technology. Technology may become so advanced you lose your ability to make complete use of it. Ask God for the miracle of wisdom. Use what God gives you wisely.

"Who is like the wise? Who knows the explanation of things? A person's wisdom brightens their face and changes its hard appearance" (Ecclesiastes 8:1 NIV).

Day 17

Pray for a sound mind all the days of your life. Having a sound mind may not seem important. Walk down the hallway of a nursing home and see the people. Many people, once productive, have lost their capabilities. People with minds gone because of Alzheimer's disease, dementia, or senility, just to name a few diseases. Young people are also struck with diseases. Your mind in a technology-based society must be sound, as devices become more complex and more is asked of you daily. Ask God for the miracle of a sound mind as you go into the future. God can give us that miracle.

It is a gift of God to have a sound mind. Every day, you expect to have a sound mind. A sudden fall or automobile accident can take that away quickly. You don't like to think about it, but diseases can also take your sound mind away. Thank God for your sound mind, or you could not read this book (or any book). Take nothing away from those who have suffered the loss of a sound mind; they are still to be loved and cherished deeply. Your own mind must be protected daily with prayer. Ask God for the miracle of a sound mind. Ask for that miracle to take place.

"For God has not given us a spirit of fear, but of power, and of love and of a sound mind" (2 Timothy 1:7 KJV).

Day 18

Pray for the ability to survive in a world you cannot predict. We live in uncertain times; the world could turn dreadful. You may someday need the miracle to be able to survive. Ask God to watch over you constantly, and ask him to be with you if such a time were to come. Society could break down due to foreign invasion or civil unrest or some disaster that you cannot imagine, such as an earthquake or great storm. Even if survival is necessary for a short time until you are rescued, pray for God to be there with you. In the darkest hours of life, you need him most, and a miracle can help you when nothing else can. Pray for that miracle now, before anything like that happens.

You might wonder every day what could go wrong. A short power outage can be very disruptive. Imagine not having water or a roof over your head as well. How far are you from needing to survive? Prepare your skills, equipment, and supplies. Be as ready as you can, and know where to go in case of any emergency. There may be times when staying inside in your home is the best. Pray for God to tell you in some way. Ask for the miracle of survival now and in the techno world to come. You may rely on others even more in that day so be kind to others.

"Do not forsake me, O lord, O my God, be not far from me!" (Psalm 38:21 NKJV).

Day 19

Ask God to give you the miracle of not being overwhelmed by things that happen beyond your control. Whatever happens, God can give you power at that moment to handle whatever it is. When you come upon an auto accident, you want to help but may believe that somebody else would do better. When someone falls to the ground, it could be seconds or minutes that save their lives. Stop and help; you may be the first line of defense at that moment. Do not be overwhelmed; ask God for that miracle.

Nobody wants to help, lest they get involved. A child rides his bicycle into the street and gets hit by a car; you drive off. You may run the risk that someone you help may still die. But maybe they will say thank you, if you save their life. Pray God will give you the strength to overcome your doubts and fears when the need arises. He will be there with you. Believe you are not alone. God will help you, so be his hands, be his help; you will not be alone. Ask for the miracle of strength, regardless of the situation. Let God be the miracle maker and do not be overwhelmed.

"Therefore, if the Son makes you free, you shall be free indeed" (John 8:36 NKJV).

Day 20

The world that lies ahead of us quite likely will use robotic mechanisms. Robots could be smarter and stronger than we are. Personal robots may turn against us. The future of hacking will need to be dealt with, lest a robotic machine turn against us. Without a doubt, you will need a miracle. Robotic soldiers may soon be ready to wage war; you cannot know the future. The miracle you will need is personal protection from whatever form of techno device you might face. May God give you the miracle of personal protection.

You may be relatively safe today, but you may face someone intent on robbing you or causing you great harm using technology. The miracle to be protected not only applies to the future but now, in your everyday life. This one miracle alone is certainly worth asking God for. You must ask almighty God to protect you as you go about your daily life. The future will belong to God, as it does today. Ask God for the miracle of technology protection. Ask God to protect your technology that it be not hacked or destroyed or stolen or compromised in any way.

"But I will sing of your strength, in the morning I will sing of your love, for you are my fortress, my refuge in times of trouble" (Psalm 59:16 NIV).

Day 21

When you think of traffic, you usually think of a large metropolitan city with lots of cars. Highways are quite often a place where you spend hours at a time every day. When you go to public places, you are often stuck in lines that require you to wait for long periods of time. What miracle can you ask for to help you with such problems? Let us pray to God for the miracle of patience.

Until we have solved the problem of traffic and waiting in lines, we will need patience. Even if you are fortunate and drive an automobile that directs itself around traffic, you will need patience. The miracle of patience is one you can use to your advantage. Someday, you may have driverless cars and holographic images to help you to do business. But for now, experience the waiting time to pray and ask God for more miracles. We hope that technology can solve the problem for us somehow, but until that time comes, you will need patience and lots of it. When you are stuck in traffic, use that time wisely to speak to God. Pray for a miracle of some kind at this opportune moment given to you. Use any free time to pray for miracles God can still hear.

"But they that wait upon the Lord shall renew their strength, they shall mount up with wings as eagles, they shall run, and not be weary, and they shall walk, and not faint" (Isaiah 40:31 KJV).

Day 22

We need the miracle of power over fear every day. For some people, fear is such a major problem that they cannot leave their house. Phobias are prevalent, from fear of heights to fear of marketplaces. Fear of germs creates a yoke of bondage upon people that is as crippling as any disease. You may not have a phobia but may know others who do. Pray for the miracle of overcoming phobias for yourself and others. If you have a phobia, pray that God will perform a miracle and remove it totally.

Some people are afraid to fly. Others may be able to fly with medications but still have a difficult flight. The awesome power of a jet engine is amazing; it is a beast on the wing that is strong enough to easily carry passengers. Many miracles apply to fears, so pray to be released from ever having such fears and pray for those who have any kind of phobia. It is difficult to comprehend the suffering that can take place in the minds of a phobic. If you know someone who is phobic, talk to them and pray for them; counsel them and pray for a miracle.

"Now will I break his yoke from off thee, and burst thy bonds in sunder" (Nahum 1:13 KJV).

Day 23

Pray to God to give you the miracle over pain. Your body aches, sometimes in ways you do not even know. You get tired and exhausted. You suffer pain because of injuries or surgery; the pain can be overwhelming. Once the surgery is over, you need recovery time to get back to a normal lifestyle, but you still have pain. You may suffer severe injuries or pain in your muscles or joints from your work or play. You need a miracle when you have pain, not just pills that lead to addiction.

You don't know the future and what technology can bring as far as curing your pain. Pray that God will give us the technology to rid you of the pain quickly. Pain injections may only work temporarily. Headaches are only one common kind of pain. Pray not just for technology to save you but pray that a miracle will take place that eliminates your pain. Ask God for the miracle of pain relief. This may not seem like a miracle but if you are in agonizing pain you need a miracle.

"He performs wonders that cannot be fathomed, miracles that cannot be counted" (Job 9:10 NIV).

Day 24

When we ask for a miracle, we often doubt that God will hear us. In the case of this miracle, it may be difficult to believe that it is possible. I speak of the miracle of the cure for cancer. This disease is fast becoming the number one killer of people young and old. You may not believe that God will provide healing and eradication of this disease. Yet in the past, people did not think a cure for AIDS was possible. Great strides have been made in curing AIDS; patients are living much longer. Other diseases such as tuberculosis and leprosy were likely thought as incurable.

We often forget that all things are possible with God's help. You may know people who have passed on because of cancer. You may be suffering from cancer even as you read this. Believe that God can cure that ailment. If family members, coworkers, or friends have this disease, help them to believe. Pray for them and pray for God's miracle to come forth. Researchers are working feverishly to rid the world of this disease, so pray they will be successful. God's healing power can go beyond science and heal when it seems hopeless. Miracles abound in the Bible, yet many were scoffers. Put your belief ahead of your doubting; let God create a breakthrough and heal those who need his healing today. The day may come when we see many diseases eradicated. Technology is helping us find cures for diseases within our genetic structure. Stem cell research and other methods are being used. Many people are being cured today that never expected to be healthy again. Many had given up hope, only to find that their illness was now in remission. The most difficult patients to watch are children who fight the battle in heroic fashion. Who would ever think a child would get something so devastating and so young, yet there are far too many of them under treatment in hospitals today. Pray for those adults and children who have no financial program to help them. Pray for those who do not have someone to help them get a glass of water when they are too weak to get it themselves. Our technology is wonderful, but it needs to move against diseases like cancer and let people live out their lives comfortably. Thank God for those who have been healed, for he is the great healer. Thank God for those who help the afflicted for they should be given much thanks. Ask for the miracle to overcome cancer today. Ultrasound and other methods of noninvasive surgery are now being performed; tumors are being surgically removed from the body right now. This is only the beginning. Pray for the miracle of a total cure for any kind of cancer. The greatness of this miracle staggers the mind that it would be possible. God can do all things all things. Believe in the miracle of Gods healing power over any disease.

"Yea, though I walk through the valley of the shadow of death, I will fear no evil: for thou art with me; thy rod and thy staff they comfort me" (Psalm 23:4 KJV).

Day 25

There is a moment that none of us wish to face. You may have faced it already, or you may be in some part of that situation at this moment. Nobody can feel what happens in that moment. In the darkest of times, you may need a miracle. But you must realize that you are never alone, no matter what your body tells you. You do not have the capacity to see God's presence near you. When the time comes and you are alone and frightened, realize he is there. Do not rely on your hearing or eyesight; believe he is there beyond your physical senses. You may feel powerless and afraid with what has happened. You may even have a cell phone, but it cannot bring you peace. God can. If you are in an emergency situation, call 911, but then reach out to God. Reach for the miracle that overcomes your darkest and most difficult hour. There are people who care about you, regardless of what you may think. Only God's true peace can reach within you and calm you down. When you are in a panic, begin to speak to God; don't let yourself become hysterical. Don't look within yourself; look outward and upward to God, and ask for that miracle that delivers you through the darkness.

We tend to live our lives in a steady pattern, hoping that every day will be safe and that nothing will happen. Those moments are when God is there. We do not control all things; we are just mortals subject to events that happen. We all need God, whether it is an auto accident or some other event. We may tend to forget God in that hour and even blame him, but that is the worst thing you can do. Use technology to help you. Call 911 if it is a situation that they can help you with. Calling 911 may just save your life. Regardless, cry out to God until they arrive, and if 911 cannot help, you still have God to rely on. Don't forget any options you might have open to you. Call somebody, just anybody you know; the sound of their voice can calm you. Keep asking God for that miracle. Cry out for that miracle that comes to you in the darkest hour. God is above all things; he is a God of love. Pray without ceasing and ask God for the answer. Be patient and strong with God's help. God's presence can bring you peace and that peace can bring you through anything. Miracles at times like these can be very real if you will allow God to be present with you and comfort you.

"Peace I leave with you, my peace I give unto you; not as the world giveth, I give unto you. Let not your heart be troubled, neither let it be afraid" (John 14:27 KJV).

Day 26

When you are young, you may be unsure of yourself. You may think you must constantly prove that you are good enough. As you age, you may feel more confident; you may become so confident you feel you can do anything or go anywhere. The world is yours, for a few years. Then as you become elderly, you may feel less than adequate, as if the world is going way too fast and you wish it would slow down. Elderly people often feel there is too much technology and it is far too complicated. You often hear the words as you go through life: "That's not good enough." You begin to wonder about yourself as you see others who seem to be good enough; they are honored by award ceremonies in the workplace or community. You may doubt yourself even more when others succeed. For the most part, you believe in yourself, but perhaps not strongly enough. You may need the miracle of confidence. Learn to believe in yourself and believe that nobody can stop you. The miracle of believing that you can accomplish anything is an amazing gift. Ask for this miracle to come upon you; it can be a great friend.

If you believe those who say, "That's not good enough," you are using a measuring stick of their choice. It's not a measure of who you are. Realize that you can make your own measuring stick. It is measuring yourself that is the problem. All too often, you may believe what others say. People can be very cruel and may not realize how deeply they hurt you with words. Parents and relatives can carry much weight when they belittle you or place a sibling above you. We all develop at a different pace. Muscles that didn't work in middle school may decide to become active later; by high school, you may be nearly ready for the Olympics. One of the deadliest things you can do to people is destroy their confidence. Once your confidence is gone, you accept who you are. That is just your place in life, but that is not true. Drug dealers often use this approach to make someone believe drugs can make them happy or stronger. Seek God for the miracle of confidence. Seek for that confidence that can carry you through life, and help others restore their confidence. You can soar beyond your expectations and watch as others try to make you doubt yourself. With the miracle of receiving God's confidence, it will stay for life. Give God the credit as you use God's miracle of confidence, and use his measuring stick. It's unlimited in what you can do. Pray for the miracle of confidence.

"Let us then approach God's throne of grace with confidence, so that we may receive mercy and find grace to help us in our time of need" (Hebrews 4:16 NIV).

Day 27

Pray for the little children in the world. Pray for a miracle to protect all the little children all over the world. Both boys and girls need protection in this world. In some parts of the world, little girls are killed at birth; little girls and boys are too often sold into prostitution at an early age. Some children are killed for their organs so the family can eat and survive a little longer. The miracle of child protection is needed in a technological civilization. They deserve better than we have given them in the past.

We need to pray for children worldwide to be protected from people that would use children for their own purpose. Children cannot protect themselves and must rely on adults to help them and protect them. Children are not a commodity like cattle to be harvested and sold for financial gain. Pray for a miracle of protection that will come upon the little children of the world, for such is the kingdom of heaven. Children may not even know how to ask God for a miracle. Teach little children to pray whenever possible. Pray for a miracle to take place that protects them.

"All things whatsoever ye would that men should do to you, do ye even so to them: for this is the law and the prophets" (Matthew 7:12 KJV).

Day 28

Today, somewhere, a surgery will take place in some hospital or surgical center. We need to pray for the miracle of a successful surgery to take place. Doctors train for many years to become able to perform a surgery, and nurses, anesthesiologists, and assistants are trained as well. Patients go into the surgery knowing the risks, but they need a miracle. Most patients are frightened as they enter the surgery room; pray for them to be calm. Patients need a miracle from God to survive the surgery, and with God's help, that will happen.

We need to pray for the miracle of a successful surgery. Pray for whatever surgery is taking place; it isn't necessary to know who or where, just that they need a miracle, so ask God for that miracle. Pray that God will prepare the surgery room and sterilize it of any dangerous bacteria that could be present. We need to pray for doctors to be of a sound mind and not have something happen before the surgery that distracts them from what they are about to do. Pray that God will help the doctor to be prepared mentally and physically for that surgery. Some surgeries take longer and require much more energy; pray the doctor will be ready when the surgery begins and have the strength to finish properly. Pray that nothing will happen during the surgery, such as an emergency call which might take the doctor away. Pray that doctors will successfully perform the surgery to the best of their ability; if something is found inside the patient, pray the doctor can repair it and the entire surgery will be completed. Pray for the doctor's strength to return to them following this surgery. Pray for the anesthesiologist to be prepared as well before the surgery, both mentally and physically, and that no disruptions will occur for them. Pray that they will be attentive during the surgery and that they will be skillful at what they do, constantly monitoring any fluctuations in the patient's vital signs. Pray that the anesthesiologist knows when to add or decrease the proper medications during the surgery and that they will help the patient to recover properly from the surgery. Pray for the assistants and nurses to be attentive and involved throughout the entire surgery, that they will be mentally and physically able to do their individual jobs as well. Pray that the patient will be prepared to go through the surgery and will have strength to handle any unforeseen dangers. Pray for the instruments to be sanitized and all equipment to work properly. Pray for the recovery team to be able to handle any emergencies as well. Wherever technology is involved, pray it will not fail. Finally, pray for God's presence to be in the room, guiding and directing everything, and that the miracle of a successful surgery will take place and the outcome (including recovery of the patient) will be successful. Pray for the miracle of a successful surgery.

"Don't fear, because I am with you; don't be afraid, for I am your God. I will strengthen you, I will surely help you; I will hold you with my righteous strong hand" (Isaiah 41:10 CEB).

Day 29

Whenever you get on an airplane, you take for granted that you will have a safe flight. The pilot and crew have been trained, and mechanics have checked the plane while it is on the ground. The plane is properly fueled, so what could go wrong? Airplanes not only fly; they literally fly themselves for much of the time. Instruments control most everything on the plane, and the cockpit gauges reflect our technology; But regardless of technology, the pilot must fly the plane, and so we must ask for the miracle of a safe flight.

Scientists are working hard, but we do not yet have pilotless airplanes. We need to pray for pilots and crew members. We need to pray that they are sober and of a sound mind. Pray that their minds are not disrupted by personal problems or medical issues. We need to pray that all passengers will be at peace and nobody will disrupt the flight with a weapon; we must pray that weather will not be a problem. We need to pray that the plane operates as it should, and the engines need to work well, and the take-off and landing are safe. Pray for the miracle of a safe flight.

"In peace, I will lie down and sleep for you alone, LORD, make me dwell in safety" (Psalm 4:8 NIV).

Day 30

Pray for the miracle to be able to perform your job in such a way as to receive a promotion, recognition, or even a new job. Not everyone is employed; if you are not employed, then pray for someone close to you to receive this miracle. If not for yourself, pray for a family member or neighbor or friend. Jobs are difficult to find nowadays, but those who have jobs may need help in some aspect of their work. Pray for the miracle of job success that will surpass your present situation. God does not mean for us to struggle endlessly; pray for his help.

You may take your job for granted and assume it will always be there. Many companies are downsizing or cutting back. Job security is a blessing. To be recognized as a good employee is a miracle. Promotions and pay raises happen. New jobs become available, and with God's timing, you may just happen to find a better position. Experience is a good teacher. Look for ads in newspapers and online, but before you move to another company, make sure it has stability. If possible, leave the door open to your old job (if it is adequate); you may need it. Pray for the miracle of job success and that you make the right decision on keeping your present job or taking a new job.

"Though thy beginning was small, yet thy latter end should greatly increase" (Job 8:7 KJV).

Day 31

Today, situations may arise where you need the help of a policeman, fireman, or emergency service people to protect and help you, whether it be from an auto accident, a fire, or a medical emergency. Without these people in place, a lawless society could threaten your life. Such situations could cause us to become like a third world country. It would be difficult to keep items you rely on, such as cell phones and computers, without adequate help. Criminals would take from the weak and those not strong enough to protect themselves; your desire to own valuable items would be reduced, knowing you could not afford to replace such items if they were stolen. We need the miracle of a society that can protect its own people. Men and women who wear those uniforms need our prayers as well; they are often killed in the line of duty. Pray that those men and women have no malice in their heart toward anyone and that all races, religions, sexes, ages, and colors will be treated fairly, with the help of a mighty God.

If you are walking down the street and are confronted by someone with criminal intent, you want to be able to call for help. In some countries, governments do not respond as well as ours. You need to encourage people who help you in situations that arise; you may seriously need their help. Perhaps a fireman pries open your car door after an accident so you can escape. You might not be appreciative of the rescue; you need to be truly grateful when you receive help from one of these people. They train hard and place their own lives at risk for a paycheck that pays the bills, and that's about it. Society may be growing in science and technological devices, but there is no point in moving forward only to return home and find all your expensive devices stolen. Pray that the men and women who protect us have a good attitude, in which we are all equally important, and pray they will help us because they want to help us. Thank them for their service, and realize they are a part of the technology and protection loop. They may well save your life; they could be your first line of defense. Pray that their technology works well on their ambulances and other emergency vehicles. Technology devices can identify who you are and save your life, while respecting your privacy. Future technology must involve our public servants; pray that it does. We have made many advances in society, but we cannot afford bodyguards and medically proficient people to go everywhere we go. Pray God's presence to be with you and that you will be blessed with protection. Pray for the miracle of protection wherever you go, and pray that those who perform such duties be safe as well.

"But the Lord is faithful, and he will strengthen you and protect you from the evil one" (2 Thessalonians 3:3NIV).

Day 32

As you go through life, one of the worst enemies you face is yourself. You may get upset over things you wish didn't bother you, but they still annoy you. You may look at the world in a gloomy sort of way, wondering when things are going to get better. The world has changed, and it's not going to get any better, you may think. You need to ask for a miracle. The miracle you need is the miracle to overcome depression in any form. You need to change your outlook on life. Yesterday's history, tomorrow's a mystery, today is a gift, that's why they call it the present. It is truly a gift from God. You need a miracle that helps you in a way that nothing else can. You need a miracle that fits your life, and furthermore, it needs to be something you deserve. You need to look at the events of the past in a different way. You need to stop looking at the past like it's your enemy; it has prepared you for today and tomorrow. It may have caused you a lot of trouble, but it's over now. You need some changes to take place. You need a smile on your face, laughter in your heart, cheerfulness in your voice, and joy in your spirit. You need a miracle that lifts you up above all your past troubles. You need a miracle that lifts you up above the past and present and beyond into the future, which will be without problems. You need a miracle to overcome depression of any kind.

You need to let go of the past, even if it does belong to you. You need to let go of that which causes you problems. By turning it over to God and asking for the miracle of your spirit being lifted, you can overcome any problem. You must first believe he can help you;

second, believe that if you but ask God, he will help you. Leave the troubles of the world in God's hands. The past is what it is; you cannot change it, but you can change the present. Your past has caused you more than enough trouble. You can change your future by acting on it now. You need to live now and into the future, as though you are punishing your past for what it has done to you. It is as if your past were a small thing that grew into a problem you didn't expect. Regardless of the good things that have happened, problems may have woven themselves into your life. Whatever has hurt you, caused you to be upset, or created misery in your life needs to go away. Decide for yourself if you have had enough of your problems; if the answer is yes, then you need a miracle. You need the miracle of your spirit being raised up above all your problems. Be raised up above your past and above that which has dug its way into your life and made itself at home. It is not of God, but God can make it go away. With God's help, it will go away. Your memories will be there, but their power over you will be replaced by God's miracle of a spirit raised up in joy and happiness. It may have even affected your health; ask God to heal any ailment caused by your troubled past.

You need to make the bad past go away, but let any good memories stay. Be watchful that the past won't come back; it has found a home, and whatever is troublesome to you has had its day, so let go of it completely. Accept the joy that only God can give you. In the joy that God gives, let the past fade away. You need not be angry about the past; those things happened, so just know they caused you pain. Nobody wants you to have that pain. What was happening before you was so subtle, it seemed natural, but that is not true. God's joy is natural, so receive his natural joy and happiness. Be filled in your spirit above your past and present problems, and know God brings freedom with his natural joy.

Being raised up in spirit by God can bring joy you may not have had since you were a child. Your health may even improve because when you are upset, your body can react in the wrong way. Let that joy spring up and even run over, and let today be the first beautiful day you've had in a very long time. Make it a very beautiful, happy day. Let nobody take that joy away from you again. Ask for the miracle to be raised up in spirit, and live your life with unspeakable joy, full of God's glory. What seemed impossible is possible with the help of God. Travel somewhere or do something you always wanted to do. Do something nice for yourself. This may be the one more miracle you have needed for a long time; ask God to help you overcome depression.

"And David danced before the Lord with all his might; and David was girded with a linen ephod" (2 Samuel 6:14 KJV).

Day 33

Let go. That is the way to pray to God for a miracle. If you try to maintain control over every miracle, it's as if you want to do God's job for him. It's like saying he doesn't exist, so you'll pretend. A true miracle comes from God freely because you ask him for it. You can soar upward like an eagle, and you can let your body rest in the peace that only he can give. Your physical self needs to rest in a deep, restful sleep as you pray, believing God hears you. It can be difficult for you in a technological world to let go; you need to be the one in charge of search engines and websites and all that the Internet may offer. God's world is beyond technology, even though that seems difficult to believe. You were made by an omniscient God, and you don't need to know everything. You need the miracle of letting go and letting God, within your physical self. As you let go within yourself, you may feel your problems go away. Be lifted upward and lose yourself, in a heavenly way, toward God. Problems may lose their power over you, and peace may come upon you. Ask that the miracle of letting go and letting God brings his peace to your physical body, not just in your spirit. Your physical body needs to rest and feel comfort in God's love and warmth. Your daily life is not easy, unless you make it easy for yourself. Many people can find happiness and peace without God, it would seem, but sooner or later, they need God's help. You need help constantly, and God provides that help if you but seek him.

Within yourself, you can become tired and discouraged. You may even think there's no use in trying. People become so discouraged, they sometimes want to harm themselves. It's as if you are carrying a load of rocks on your back. Empty that load of rocks into God's hands. Just imagine yourself carrying a bag of rocks. By yourself, you could easily tire under the weight. You may be the type who wants to help others and carry their problems as well as your own. Letting go and letting God carry the load is itself a miracle. God tells you to love others as yourself, but he doesn't require you to carry their load. You may be helping someone because they have a drug or alcohol problem, and they do need help. But imagine if you were to begin praying for them differently, by asking God to carry them. Do not be their God in any way. Learn to get out of God's way. Let God carry your load of problems and receive the miracle of Gods peace upon yourself as the weight of trying to carry others is lifted off of you.

"Jesus looked at them and said, 'With man this is impossible, but with God, all things are possible'" (Mark 10:27 NIV).

Day 34

Ahead of you lies the future. When you think of the future, you may think of yourself first, such as where you will be and what will you be doing. Eventually, you will get around to realizing that your future may be about inventions and technology. Some inventions will come from companies that exist now; others will arise up out of our imagination and dreams. Some inventions will come from individuals with lots of ideas. A beautiful future may lie just ahead of you. Can you integrate with one another as you integrate technology and new ideas into your life each day? You need the miracle of a future that is safe; your technology may be guarded in such a way that you don't worry about those who would steal from you or harm you. You need the miracle of a world in which technology brings you comfort and convenience; that is a world you can only dream will exist. It will be a beautiful world. With God's help, it will come to pass; with God's help, your future will be as beautiful as a sunset.

We are a unique people, in that what science fiction writers once imagined, we now enjoy. We seem to have distanced ourselves from every species on earth. We as a species have not truly come together as one yet as we thrive in our technology. We need God's miracle to help us create a beautiful world that will make us more productive and more comfortable and safer than we have ever been. We need each other and the love each of us can give. We need a renaissance world in which all of us can contribute something in our own way. We have always had to focus on food production or jobs or commuting or worry about crime or disease. We are an artistic, beautiful species, unlike any other, and we need the help of God to become more beautiful than ever. We need to be able to rely on each other and look to one another for help and assistance. People we barely know surprise us with what they know once we get to know them. That person could be the next Einstein, and with your help, you might just create an invention that helps everyone have a more beautiful world. Look to God for the miracle of a beautiful future. Birds fly in a flock, side by side, yet never bump into each other. Schools of fish glide through the waters with their beautiful colors and turn easily, as if they are one. Imagine what you can do if you but look to God and become as one with him and each other. Ask God for the miracle of a beautiful and safe future as together we conquer the future. The future we pray will become a great miracle.

"And thou shalt love the lord thy God with all thy heart, and with all thy soul, and with all thy mind, and with all thy strength: this is the first commandment. And the second is like, namely this. Thou shalt love thy neighbor as thyself. There is none other commandment greater than these" (Mark 12:30–31 KJV).

Day 35

Pray for the miracle of finding a life partner. We all need someone to be with us. We need someone around us who truly cares for us, who knows our strengths and weaknesses and can forgive us when we fail. People who have been married a long time have developed a system where they live around each other, doing things for one another, surprising one another, and loving one another. It used to be common for people to find one life partner, but now people tend to have several partners in life; one day, they meet someone different, and there is no question about whether this is the right person. Ask for the miracle of a life partner, and if you already have a life partner, ask God to bless him or her.

I have lived with the same person almost sixty years. Each of us supports the other. It's something I truly want to do every day. I have been supported mentally, physically, and spiritually, as well as psychologically. I have gone through some dark hours where I did not believe I would live, but it turned out all right. I have no doubt that God hears your prayers as well as those of people who love you. I have believed in miracles almost all my life and can truly say God has performed miracles that have absolutely amazed me. I am not worthy to receive a miracle, but God performed them anyway. Don't call something a miracle while you're going through it; it's not until later that you look back and realize you just went through a miracle. If something happens that should have taken your life and it didn't, that's a miracle. People may wonder how you survived through that surgery or accident or illness. The truth is, I would not have, except for God. I cannot count the miracles God has done for me, but they are many, and I thank him for each of them.

A life partner who prays for you is one of your most valuable assets (although looking for a life partner is not like panning for gold). The prayers of a life partner are heard by God quite often and it may be that it's the tears that go with the prayers makes God hear. For many reasons, the miracle of finding a life partner is one of the most satisfying miracles there is. Pray sincerely to meet the right person, and let the miracle begin. Do not expect the miracle to be obvious when looking for a life partner. They come from places you never expect then suddenly you just know that person is the right one. The feeling of finding a life partner is like no other experience in the world. You don't become wealthy yet you feel great wealth. You don't feel like you just became famous yet both of you look to each other as though nobody else exists. This miracle alone can be a goldmine for life as together you face every problem imaginable together and overcome each problem one by one. What a joy to find a life partner. What a miracle it is. May God bless your miracle of finding a life partner.

"What therefore God hath joined together, let no man put asunder" (Mark 10:9 KJV).

Day 36

Let us pray today for a miracle on behalf of our military and police officers as well as our firefighters and rescue workers. These are the people who place their lives on the line every day on our behalf; sometimes, they lose their lives trying to rescue or protect us. You deserve to be protected, and for the most part, God does protect you, but you often hear of people being rescued by one of these people. Men and women place their lives on the line just to save the life of someone else; too often, they are injured or even killed in the line of duty. They need a miracle from God every day to help them solve each situation. Military people go to war and get shot at or killed in the line of duty. They are often injured or killed in training. Pray for God to send them a miracle and so they can protect or rescue you should you ever need such protection.

You may be so used to having these people there when you need them that you never think about them. Third world countries envy who we have protecting and rescuing us. These men and women are especially fine people. We are blessed of God to have these people helping us. Did God perform a miracle to create this system to protect us? Are we looking at a miracle in progress or waiting for them to be involved in a miracle? Talk to these people and ask if they believe in miracles. They might say they rely on miracles every single day. The miracle that extends to these brave people applies to you and me. If you but believe as they do, that they are being watched over, you will do well. They must ask God to help them regardless of the weather or circumstances; too often, it is unexpected. Firefighters face an unpredictable force when they enter a burning building, but many of them welcome the challenge and turn the mission over to God. It is this blind faith that moves humanity forward, and with technology, these men and women can know much more about the situations they face ahead of time. We see the heroic help of technology being blended together with God's miracle help, and what better example do we need that technology and God work together? Your pathway may not have a light before you, and unlike the men and women who protect and rescue us, we do not know what we face when we go out the door. Technology may help tell us if there is an accident up ahead; that is helpful, but technology needs to come to the forefront for all of us to be protected. You need the protection of God, as do those who are our protectors. You need God in case there is a need for a miracle. Look to God as you buckle your seat belt, and ask God for your miracle. Remember: Those men and women in prayer are sworn to protect you. They need a miracle.

"Greater love hath no man than this, that he lay down his life for his friends" (John 15:13 KJV).

Day 37

Pray for the miracle of finding understanding: not only understanding God's word but your own world, the world you live in, and the world of people and technology. Pray you will find a mentor who knows God, who can guide you through the deep waters that lie ahead in your life; they may be the most beautiful days. Pray to find someone who understands the way God hears and answers prayer. Some people are gifted of God so that when something happens, others call them if they need a prayer. Pray for a person who understands the Bible and knows how the Old and New Testament go together. To get to the point where you understand the Bible by yourself may take a very long time. Why not ask for help? Otherwise, it may be years until it is second nature to you.

The Bible is filled with people who received miracles that came to them unexpectedly. To pick up the Bible and start to read it may be overwhelming by yourself, whereas others may carry it with them everywhere they go. The combination of a mentor and your Bible can be an awesome experience. First find a person you can relate to who can tell you about their experience with the word of God. It may not fit what you think the Bible says, but move on to the next mentor until you find one who understands what you seek. Perhaps you can find a pastor or deacon or someone you consider very well educated. It is not that the Bible is a college course, but it can be researched over and over as you find new understandings every day. Do not miss this magnificent side of what God has in store for you.

Your opinion of the Bible may be very different today than it will be a year from now or ten years from now. Don't be afraid to ask your mentor the most absurd questions about why something happened in the Bible. Don't be afraid to ask them the most intimate questions you can about any person you choose. You may end up getting more of an opinion than you expected. Learn but form your own opinions.

When you have reached a point where you feel you have your own idea what the Bible says, reach out using the Internet or newspaper or maybe a friend to find a church that believes close to what you believe. Study the beliefs of that church as much as possible. Do as much research as possible before you join, but attend a church near you and seek fellowship there. Fellowship can be one of the most important aspects of the church. Continue to ask God for miracles every day and build your faith brick by brick, until you feel God is there with you and will answer your prayer.

This miracle could really help you, and I hope that it does. If you were in college or training for a job, you would study to understand that course. The Bible cannot be placed into a single category, but it is like an on-the-job-training program filled with wonderful discoveries. It is like fiction, but it is not fiction. It may seem like the most boring book you've ever read until one day, you see something in the Bible, and a light goes on. Look for that light that goes on in your mind. Look for the light that opens your mind to a place you never knew existed. Look for that secret door that is there, and find a new beginning and a new purpose for living. Technology is wonderful, and through research, you can find websites that provide all kinds of information. Through some websites, you can find people who can help you with your questions and walk you through answers to those questions in a simple, easy way.

Some people in the Bible will fascinate you; by looking deep into individual people in the Bible, you will learn more about yourself. Some people in the Bible made ridiculous mistakes; some went to the mountaintop. Choose a person and let that person come alive out of the pages of the Bible and learn from them. If that person were alive today, what would he or she say about technology or some other subject? How would you respond by yourself in the world they lived in? Learn more about their world through websites about the customs and lifestyles of those people. Could you survive without technology at that time? Find where you might have enjoyed living in the Bible and who you would want to be your friends. Where would you be comfortable? Study about Jesus and his miracles, and see that God not only performs miracles but promises us that if he goes to the Father, we can even do greater things than these. Pray for the miracle of understanding what God would have you know. Study to find strength and faith in the Bible; talk to others more knowledgeable than yourself, who have experienced what it means to have faith in God. You may find by learning more about the Bible that believing is easier than you thought; you can then comfortably ask God for a miracle and not doubt that he will hear you. Learn that you can ask for a miracle, and God will hear that request, and you will see changes in your life and the world around you. You need not seek these things but know that God still hears your prayers so at least hang onto that belief in miracles. God hears all prayers. There are no dumb prayer requests. God knows our hearts and minds and needs.

"Study to shew thyself approved unto God, a workman that needeth not to be ashamed, rightly dividing the word of truth" (2 Timothy 2:15 KJV).

Day 38

This miracle to pray for is for you. It should apply to all the people you meet wherever you go. If you can find this miracle and take it into your spirit, it could change your life. It is a special miracle, in that it touches so many areas of your life and the lives of your friends and those you meet today, tomorrow, and forever. Ask God for the miracle of gentleness. At first, it may sound like something you do if you have a baby; you are careful not to hurt it and end up talking and singing to it, then the baby smiles at you and goes to sleep in your arms. That is part of the miracle of gentleness. I pray that you will ask God for this miracle; you may find that a gentleness comes upon you as well as a peace that passes your understanding of what peace is. You will feel a change taking place within.

When you pray for the miracle of gentleness, let it come upon you physically; you can feel a relaxation come upon you that makes your face relax as well as all its features. Let your facial muscles relax around your eyes and even behind your eyes, deep into its sockets. Then let the tension go out of your jaw and let those jaw muscles relax. Let your mouth and lips and tongue relax; let all that tension leave your face and behind your head, into your neck. If you allow God to perform this miracle, as you do feel the tension leave your body, you may realize a part of him that is unknown to you. God is gentle yet able to fling the stars into space. He cares for you when you could not believe yet he does care because somehow you deserve it.

It is not just that you are being protected by God, but his love comes onto you as he takes away every tear and tension within. Welcome him into yourself as you would accept sleep; you may ask God for this miracle to help you sleep. Do not do this while driving. You can spread this feeling all the way to your toes and legs and hips until your whole body is in God's hand, safe and secure.

The miracle of gentleness is like a soft warm breeze that blows across you, softening all your anger. When you touch the face of the one you love, let the softest touch of your hand reach out to them. Speak to them in a gentle, loving tone that says you care for them as God cares for you. Let your hands touch like a feather touches the wind and float along into the warmth of the sun. When you step outside, listen to the sounds differently, as birds sing softly in praise to God. He has made many sounds that are beautiful to our ears when we open them to all his creation.

Feel God's love within caring for yourself but caring for others in a simple but wonderful way; maybe just saying, "How is your day going?" Try it when you check out of the grocery store or wherever you meet people working at menial jobs; they may think that nobody cares.

The time has come to remove all the tensions within you. They may have found their way into your life a long time ago, when you were a child or in school. Your reactions may have developed in such a way as to respond in a negative way. Feelings have found a home; ask these spirits to please leave. Tell them they are no longer welcome. Some people today feel they need these aggressive spirits to move people out of the way. You do not need the anger or rage that they bring.

Gentleness pushes out hatred and jealousy and a ton of things you don't need in your life; they make you old before your time. God's gentleness can move a handful of snow across a field covered in a blanket of snow frozen so hard you can barely walk in it. God may throw in a little something different to show his wonders; the ground may look almost light blue while snow dust twirls its way across a white field in the moonlight.

Feel the miracle of God's gentleness in every muscle as you relax into his wondrous world. A peace will come upon you that only he can give. Find a special place to go where you can see his wonders and just watch for the colors of a rainbow or the unmatchable beauty of a sunset as it reaches deep inside you and says everything is all right now.

You have a deep well of strength that does not need anger to fire it up. Your greatest strength comes from this deep well, filled with not only strength but power to manage your affairs and do the things you need from the energy deep within this well.

Do not let other people's voices take away your gentleness. The words and tones of others can sometimes sound like a battle cry. Other people will see your peace and gentleness, and it may make them angry. They will feel it as soon as you enter a room. They may try and stare at you, as if in a rage. Do not be moved. They are seeing and sensing something they don't have. You can talk to these people and explain what you have, but they may try and use it to their advantage, feeling that they are helping you somehow. Speak to them as Jesus did years ago, with kindness and gentleness, and keep your strength within, for from this deep well within will come decisions on everything in life. It will be based on calmness, not hysteria. Imagine a day where nothing bothers you, and the world is at peace. Imagine new friends who may last a lifetime, as you discover more of God every day. Gentleness is only the beginning of the wonders God can do in your life. Your friends, children and grandchildren will feel it and notice it, and they will be calmer too. God's wonders and rewards are endless, like the stars and beyond, to a world where someday we will meet those who have gone on before us. Ask God for the miracle of gentleness and begin the experience of a new miracle in your life the miracle of a gentle spirit.

"And let the peace of God rule in your hearts, to which also ye are called in one body, and be ye thankful" (Colossians 3:15 KJV).

Day 39

This miracle may have touched your life already many times. This miracle is one that uses technology for one of its finest purposes. The miracle you need to ask for is the miracle of music. It may seem as if you don't need a miracle to have music; just turn on your car radio or headset while you work out. No matter where you turn, there is music. The music you hear satisfies you and makes you dance or feel something inside. There are so many kinds of music; it is difficult to name them all. There are many types of instruments that can be played to produce music, and many people play those instruments. Technology plays a big part in sound reproduction and in the quality of sounds we hear. You may be connected to machines that measure your response to different types of music; again, technology is used to determine the effects of music on your body.

It seems we have covered everything with music. Music is the closest thing there is to God. In churches, music can often make parishioners feel the spirit of God. Music is part of the heavens themselves; the Bible tells us of the angels singing and playing horns, and in the sound of those horns comes the praise of God himself. Israel used horns as a call to battle, and the sound of horns became a signal to an army to charge or retreat.

Music can go deeper within yourself than you think. Music can calm you deep within, and it does this quite often. Music may have a medical benefit; you can receive healing from certain sounds, like that of the ocean or the wind. Some people use music for therapy, and through imagination, you can relax and find the world goes away when you listen to music. Music can put a baby to sleep or create a certain atmosphere with the right instrument, tone, and rhythm.

The miracle of music I speak of is one in which you are closer to God. In this closeness to God, you can feel his calmness and his love. There can be great joy in certain types of music; does music make you feel more evil or good? You can use music to make yourself feel closer to God, and that music can benefit your body, mind, and soul. Music can pull you down spiritually or lift you up. Pray for the miracle of being elevated upward by the music you hear. If you make music part of your life, you can be elevated toward God. The closer you can be to God and still be in this life and this world, the more in tune you can become with God, who made all things. If you can find music that is elevating to your spirit, then you will feel something different within. You should feel a cleansing within; you are glorifying God to the highest if you can find music that lifts you into a feeling of spiritual peace.

In some countries, a gong is used to create spiritual tones; those people believe in the various sounds of gongs. Whatever you can find for music that creates a closeness to God within you, seek it out. If you can make a problem go away with music, why not try it? It may be difficult to find music that elevates your soul, but search through the many technological pathways available to you. Once you have found that music, it will send a signal to your body that this music is the kind that will elevate your spirit; then begin to praise God as you hear it. Praising God in music is not new, but it may be new to you. You need all the help you can get; you may get very confused. Seek out music that can praise God through you. Maybe you will write words of praise or sing out praises to God. A Church may provide you with your favorite song or type of music. A Church may provide you with one of the best sources of music there is. Go to church and receive blessings from the music. Seek the miracle of music and know the joy of praising God.

"Speaking to yourselves in psalms and hymns and spiritual songs, singing and making melody in your heart to the Lord" (Ephesians 5:19 KJV).

Day 40

There is one more miracle that I feel must be included in your daily prayers, and that is the miracle of laughter. The sound of laughter is unique to humans; it is certainly a gift from God. There are moments when you want someone to tell a joke because it can remove a mountain of tension. Some people never laugh; they seem so sad. You may want to tell them, "Cheer up, it's not that bad," but for them, it is just their own personality. Some people say, "God has a sense of humor," and perhaps he does, but we know that God allows us to laugh; babies have an automatic response to laugh at certain things. Laughter seems to be the best thing you can do for yourself; it may also give you the best feeling you ever had. Once one person laughs, another person will laugh; it is contagious. The miracle of laughter in your life will be one of the greatest healers of all. If something happens to someone and you hear them laugh for the first time in a long time, you say, "It is good to hear you laugh again," and you feel the person is somehow okay. If you have not laughed in a long time, you need a miracle from God to help you restore your ability to laugh again. There is no sin in laughing (but mocking others in a cruel way or laughing at someone in a hateful way is a sin).

Scientists have done studies on laughter, but the important thing is the feeling that comes with laughter. Unrestrained, natural laughter seems like a form of music. We laugh at the strangest things, from bad jokes to the way somebody looks at us. Hearing other people laugh makes us curious and you may be curious as to what they are laughing about. You may even ask, "What's so funny?" It just seems natural to laugh; no matter where you hear it, there comes a sense of relief with it that just relaxes you, no matter how tense it may be. Seek the miracle of laughter in your own life. Ask God for the miracle of laughter; it may be one of the most satisfying of all the miracles. Don't miss an opportunity to laugh when the chance occurs. Look across a room at faces and look for the person who is smiling and smile back. Look at a baby's face and smile; even your own pet will recognize your smile or laugh. Your smile and laughter are unique to you; they are God given. Ask for more of the miracle of laughter, and enjoy this wonderful world that God has made.

"Then was our mouth filled with laughter, and our tongue with singing: then said they among the heathen, The Lord hath done great things for them" (Psalm 126:2 KJV).

Conclusion

The purpose of this book has been to give you suggestions as to ask God for a miracle. I hope that you now believe miracles can occur in your life and that you can ask God for a miracle and he can hear your prayer. We do not earn miracles; we simply place our requests before God. In his own time and through his love, he will answer us. You may be surprised at how he answers you.

If one more miracle occurs in your life because you have read this book, then to God be the praise. I only wish to glorify God; if I have offended you in any way, I apologize.

I hope you follow the forty days of prayer for a miracle and find it helps you to realize God can perform a miracle if you but pray and ask for one. These forty are just a few suggestions for miracles; add your own miracles to the list, or feel free to create a list of your own. May God richly bless you for reading this book, and may you have not just one more miracle but many miracles. May God richly bless you this day. May he bless you with many miracles or even One More Miracle this day.

Kenneth Foley

Printed in the United States
By Bookmasters